STRUCTURES OF
American Social History

Walter Nugent

Indiana University Press

BLOOMINGTON

The Samuel Paley Lectures in American Civilization, delivered at the Hebrew University of Jerusalem, February 1979 (revised and expanded).

Distributed in Israel by the Magnes Press of the Hebrew University

Manufactured in the United States of America

Library of Congress Cataloging in Publication Data

Nugent, Walter T
Structures of American social history.

Bibliography: p.
Includes index.
1. United States—Social conditions. 2. Social history. 3. United States—Population. I. Title.
HN57.N83   973   80-8634
ISBN 0-253-10356-8   1 2 3 4 5 85 84 83 82 81

To our Baby-Boomers
Kath, Rachel, Dave,
Doug, Terry, and Sou
Imagines caveant.

CONTENTS

Illustrations

PREFACE

It seems appropriate to say where this extended essay on population growth and American history came from and what it is about. As a historian of the United States, I have been fascinated for a long time with population changes, the westward movement, urbanization, immigration, transformations in agriculture, and other mass movements which make up a large part of demographic history. The history of population has always seemed to me to be basic to the history of society in all but the most elitist respects. The chance to think through the subject and make a coherent statement about it arose when, in 1977, I was honored with an invitation to deliver the Samuel Paley Lectures in American Civilization at the Hebrew University of Jerusalem.

This book is a revised and expanded version of those lectures, delivered to a general audience in the Senate Room of the Hebrew University on Giv'at Ram in February 1979 under the title "The Graying of America: Population Change and American History." It is written in the hope of making the findings of demographers and demographic historians more accessible to others. The central observation of the book may be thought-provoking for anyone: that the rate of population growth, although nearly always declining since the seventeenth century, did not drop steadily or constantly. The decline instead forms a pattern of several sudden drops from higher to lower plateaus. That pattern allows us to divide American history into periods in a new way and on a solid factual base. This book is not a full-scale demographic history, but a framework for a social history based on a demographic observation. I hope to make explicit most of the long-term trends in the history of the American population, to suggest an empirically based framework for the periodization of that history, to show how population history intertwines with social and economic history and the history of values at a number of points, and to project historical patterns into the early twenty-first century more optimistically than is usually done.

In the study of the history of population, the assumption is implicit that the mass of people are worth studying. Population history is not the history of vocal elites whose publications or letters were kept, but rather of the ill-recorded, usually voiceless majority and minorities, which, until fairly recently, were mostly rural folk. About half of them were women. Demographic history does not feature great political leaders, or industrialists, or labor leaders, or composers and writers, who in most political, economic, or cultural histories appear to have been men. Demographic history does not feature individual names at all, but deals with millions of individuals, women and men, whose interaction, measured by vital rates, forms a principal determinant of population change and hence of all other historical change.

As the book proceeds, I draw on ideas of T. R. Malthus, Frederick Jackson Turner, Fernand Braudel, and others. I take note of natural resources and their plentifulness and scarcity, and of how the rate of population growth related to decreasing availability of land over the long term. I develop the idea that most Americans over the past three centuries have lived their lives within either a frontier-rural mode or a metropolitan mode, and that American history was particularly rich, confusing, and conflict-ridden during the roughly fifty years, from about 1870 to 1920, when these two modes existed simultaneously. I conclude, extrapolating from several centuries of history, with an optimistic prognosis.

I have incurred many debts along the way, not least to the people responsible over the years for taking and compiling the United States Census, and to the demographers and historians whose works I will cite. I am greatly in the debt of Yehoshua Arieli, Shlomo Slonim, and others in the Department of American Studies of the Hebrew University of Jerusalem for inviting me to deliver the Paley Lectures for 1979. For critical readings and comments on one or another version of the entire manuscript, I am deeply grateful to Charlotte Erickson, James J. Farrell, Martin Ridge, James C. Riley, and Selwyn Troen. I also benefited from the frank comments of an anonymous reader for the Indiana University Press in 1979. Annette Atkins helped in researching various references. Several people put me on to very useful references, and they include Robert G. Barrows, Wilbur Jacobs, Sholom Kahn, John Mayer, George Stolnitz, and Paul Zall. I benefited from questions and discussions at several places where I presented aspects of the work at various stages: the audiences at the Paley Lectures themselves, in Jerusalem; the seminar on North American history of the Polish Academy of Sciences in Warsaw; lecture audiences at Hamburg University, the University of Oregon, and the Huntington Library Seminar; and members of the National Endowment for the Humanities Summer Seminar for College Teachers which I directed at Indiana in 1979. I am fully responsible, of course, for the use, misuse, or nonuse I have made of all that input.

A Fulbright-Hays senior lectureship allowed me to stay at the Hebrew University for several delightful months in 1978–79, and I thank everyone connected with that award, including Daniel M. Krauskopf, executive director of the United States–Israel Educational Foundation. I also benefited greatly from an N.E.H.–Huntington Library fellowship in 1979–80, giving me several months at the Huntington, where scholars behave as intelligent and humane conversants. Of the Huntington staff, I thank them all, but especially Ray Allen Billington, Noëlle Jackson, Virginia Renner, and Martin Ridge. I have drawn on the resources of the Huntington, the Indiana University and Hebrew University libraries, and the U.S. Cultural Center in Jerusalem. The trustees and administrators of Indiana University graciously allowed me a leave of absence and a sabbatical leave, during which I was able to visit first the easternmost frontier and then nearly the westernmost frontier of Western Civilization, in the contemplation of the history of the American population over nearly five hundred years.

Hebrew University
Jerusalem, Israel
February 1979

Huntington Library
San Marino, California
May 1980

STRUCTURES OF
American Social History

"Others appeal to history; an American appeals to prophecy; and with Malthus in one hand and a map of the back country in the other, he boldly defies us to a comparison with America as she is to be."

—Note by Frederick Jackson Turner, Turner mss., Huntington Library. Thought to be copied from *Blackwood's Magazine*, 1821.

I

America, the "New Habitat"

Short-run Observations and the Long View

After the demise of the Kennedys' Camelot and Johnson's Great Society in the early and mid-1960s, Americans became glum about their culture, its internal weaknesses, its external vulnerability, and its future. The mood at the end of the 1970s and beginning of the 1980s was querulous. National self-confidence became unfashionable. Americans expressed nostalgia for the 1950s, the days of Eisenhower and of John Foster Dulles. The uncertainty rested on well-known events which need little rehearsing. It began with the urban and campus riots of 1964 and the assassinations of the Kennedys and Martin Luther King. The Tet offensive of January 1968 seemed to brand failure on the intervention in Vietnam. Lyndon Johnson removed himself from possible reelection, for which he was eligible but which he might not have achieved. The Democratic party tore itself apart over the war issue at its nominating convention in Chicago, opening the way for Richard Nixon's ascent to the presidency. Recessions and two devaluations of the dollar reinforced uncertainty in 1970–71.

Then came Watergate, the disgrace and resignation of the Vice President in 1973 and then the President in 1974. At the same time, the Arab oil embargo quadrupled the price of a vital commodity, and the unfamiliar, half-forgotten specter of scarcity began to materialize. Between the late 1960s and 1980 the purchasing power of the dollar shrank by more than half, and inflation worsened from another doubling of world oil prices in 1979. Inflation approached 20 percent in early 1980, a level without precedent (except for a few fairly brief wartime and postwar episodes) in American history and in the history of the North Atlantic economy since the seventeenth century.[1] American self-confidence was not bolstered when Iranian revolutionaries hijacked the United States embassy in Teheran and took as hostages many of its staff. Gas lines lengthened, interest rates pushed homes beyond the reach of young adults, and a 1979 accident at a nuclear power plant in Pennsylvania threw doubts over future development of a very important and promising energy source. In the short run—if 1963 to 1980 can be called a short run—Americans had real reasons to be unhappy, for during no comparably long period, except possibly from 1800 to 1817, had they been so variously buffeted.

Uncertainty, a grasping for "relevance," hand-wringing over weaknesses perceived to exist in domestic and foreign affairs: these were marks of the public mood through much of the 1970s and into the 1980s. A noted historian of nineteenth-century America, David Herbert Donald, lamented in a New York Times Op-Ed essay that America had changed so drastically by the late 1970s that "If I teach what I believe to be the truth, I can only share with [undergraduates] my sense of the irrelevance of history, and of the bleakness of the new era we are now entering." Donald based his attitude on the end of America's traditional abundance. "From that abundance," he wrote, "we have derived our most amiable American traits— our individualism, our generosity, our incurable optimism; to it we owe our wastefulness, our extravagance, and our careless self-confidence." The past, he declared, is "today not merely irrelevant but dangerous."[2]

The *Times* printed only two rejoinders to Donald's heresy. One, from a professor of literature, affirmed that ". . . the most noble commitment is the struggle of a man to comprehend what *has* happened, to know that [as Faulkner wrote] 'the past is not dead. It is not even past.' "[3] Donald's statement was a strange one for a historian to make. But the fact that it could be uttered at all by a scholar who has thought deeply and written well of the abolitionist movement, the Civil War, and Reconstruction—hardly minor crises—underscores the seriously pessimistic mood among some of the best minds in the country, and demonstrates how thin they found the soup of the past when they strained it for sustenance to meet the future.

I take a very different position from Donald's. Despite the evidence of the events listed in the opening pages, events which gave the recent past its confining, frustrating quality and the near future its gloominess, I maintain that, when set in the proper historical context, the present situation is much less dire and collapse or even severe scarcity is much less threatening than at certain times past. Historically uninformed views of the present almost always make it appear better or worse than it really is. The historical context, the place of the recent past and the near future in time, provides stability and balance, an anchored view rather than a storm-tossed one. With Faulkner, I believe that the past remains relevant for understanding the present and for thinking intelligently about the future. Profound changes have certainly taken place in the United States, some fairly recently. But more perplexing and dangerous ones were undergone long ago. This will become clearer as we look beyond the level of events to broader patterns of historical structures and conjunctures.[4]

To see the patterns I have in mind requires looking back

over three hundred years of history. It involves a perspective unfamiliar to many people, including many historians: the development of the population of America since about 1700. I call attention to this perspective, and the patterns it reveals, not as a demographer but as a social historian making use of demographic research. These patterns speak to the broad question of where American society has been, and where it may go. The answers suggest grounds for optimism.

The rest of this chapter will be a description of three models of large-scale social change somehow relevant to America, and an observation of a demographic pattern. Did America "modernize?"[5] Was it the "first new nation?"[6] Is Turner's frontier thesis of help any more? What did Malthus conclude from American experience?[7] Consideration of these questions leads to the observation about growth rates: that Malthus was at first ignored and then, in the marketplace and without central planning, was gradually discovered and obeyed. The first chapter represents—to borrow some words of Beethoven's—the "awakening of cheerful feelings upon going out into the countryside."[8]

The second chapter introduces the main story. It sketches the demography of early modern Europe, out of which the colonial empires in the New World were founded, it focuses on the sparsely populated English colonies in the seventeenth century, and then it describes the emergence of the frontier-rural mode of life, which became standard for the majority of Americans for the next two hundred years. The third chapter describes the period from the late eighteenth century to the late nineteenth, when the frontier-rural mode dominated. These chapters are the "scene at a brook" and the "merry goings-on of the peasants."

In chapter four an alternative mode of life is seen to emerge in the early and mid-nineteenth century. When fully developed later, it deserves to be called the metropolitan mode. We also look at three "misfits"—life patterns which

stand apart from the frontier-rural or metropolitan modes—
which affected the lives of many people, but which did not
have the pervasiveness of the two main modes. These were
frontier-urban, settled-rural, and slave societies. The fourth
chapter then sketches the Great Conjuncture, the time from
about 1870 to about 1920 when the frontier-rural and metropolitan modes both flourished. The two modes, revealed by
two patterns of population change, overlapped tumultuously
for several decades, like a bad thunderstorm.

The final chapter concerns the period since 1920, when
the metropolitan mode became dominant, and it concludes
with a demographic observation about changing age structures, and some extrapolation of population history into the
early twenty-first century. That is the finale, "joyful and thank-
ful feelings after the storm."

Has America Been Unique?—
Modernization, Turner, Malthus

Many theoretical models exist to help us understand
American development and place it in the broader context of
world history, either as a humanistic exercise or in a social-
scientific pursuit of predictability. These models include,
among other possible approaches, Marxian analysis based on
class struggle, Gramsci's softening of Marxism to allow
bourgeois control by ideological hegemony rather than by
force or revolution, or classic non-Marxian social theories such
as Ferdinand Tönnies's *Gemeinschaft*-to-*Gesellschaft* shift.[9] The
list could go on. I single out modernization theory because of
its apparently growing popularity among American historians,
after its two decades of near seclusion among social scientists.
Although some historians are familiar with it to the point of
boredom or worse, evidence abounds that others are finding
modernization theory seductively attractive, some as a catch-
all term, others as something more.[10] Its most extensive appli-

cation to American history up to 1980 was Richard D. Brown's *Modernization: The Transformation of American Life, 1800–1865*, which appeared in 1976.

The term began to appear in the books and journals of sociology, political science, development economics, and social psychology in the 1950s as a crudely dichotomous and ahistorical notion that nation-states that were economically developed and politically centralized—that is, "modern"—somehow changed into modernity from a "traditional" condition. The same process was supposed to change presently underdeveloped or less-developed societies. Modernization theory has been applied at the macrolevel to whole societies or nations, mostly by political scientists and economists, and also at the microlevel of individual adjustment to social change, mostly by social psychologists.

Despite its collective authorship, spread over two decades, modernization theory has certain consistent features and meaning. Several social scientists have defined it (indeed proclaimed it) vigorously, among them Calvin Goldscheider, the team of Peter Berger and his co-authors, the micro-level analysts Alex Inkeles and David H. Smith, and a number of others.[11] Let a definition by S. N. Eisenstadt serve for all, because it is more subtle than some of the others and because Eisenstadt has been an articulate theorist of modernization since the 1950s. Eisenstadt[12] stressed the centrality of the shift from traditional to modern in societies, politics, and cultures. He recognized general agreement about the meaning of "traditional" and "modern" in classic social theory, whether in the form of Tönnies's *Gemeinschaft-Gesellschaft*, Henry Maine's status-to-contract, Durkheim's mechanical solidarity to organic solidarity, or Max Weber's traditional-charismatic to legal-rational. All involve a shift from one type of society to another. Modernization theorists have usually assumed that the shift was progressive and irreversible. In all of these theories, traditional societies were "static, with little differentiation or specialization, a predominance of mechanical division of labor, a low level of urbanization and literacy, and a strong agrarian basis as [their] main focus of population." Modern societies, on the other hand, exhibit a "very high level of differentiation, a high degree of organic division of labor specialization, urbanization, literacy and exposure to mass media, and [are] imbued with a continuous drive toward progress." In politics, modernization means a move from rule by traditionally authoritative elites to mass participation. In culture it means a shift from tradition-boundness to dynamism "oriented to change and innovation."[13] Other writers, stressing the impact of modernization on personality, and trying to identify "modernizing" traits of personality, point to a "heightened sense of personal efficacy," the urge to set the terms of one's own life, to be "relatively open-minded and cognitively flexible," as key elements.[14]

Some recent applications of modernization theory have been more subtle than earlier ones. When applied to historical events by a master of archival detail and literary grace, it seems to work convincingly, bringing a vast mass of historical data into a structured, coherent whole, yet doing no apparent violence to past social complexities. Exhibit A, in this regard, is Eugen Weber's *Peasants into Frenchmen: The Modernization of Rural France 1870–1914*.[15] In it we see, throughout the west and south of France, across most of the nineteenth century (not just after 1870), time take on new meaning, national authority spread, dialects disappear, farming commercialize, people migrate. We see the patterns of life formed by accretion over hundreds of years change from "traditional" to "modern" in only half or three-quarters of a century, and in one of the world's most developed countries. For Britain in the late eighteenth and early nineteenth centuries, the idea of modernization may also work, though its elements were captured well enough by Phyllis Deane under the more traditional rubric of "industrial revolution."[16] It may work also for other parts of Europe or for Japan. But does it work for the United States?

Certain writers have been warning that it may not, at least not in its stark, crude, early formulations. Eisenstadt himself admonished scholars to pay proper attention to "specific historical experiences" not taken into account by the modernization paradigms of the 1960s.[17] For the United States, two central problems preventing any easy application of modernization theory to its history are the lack of a traditional peasant society anything like those of preindustrial Europe or the present Middle East or Africa, and the difficulty in pointing out when, if ever, the shift from traditional to modern really happened.[18] If traditional society, and the departure from it, cannot be identified, then the usefulness of modernization theory for understanding the American experience—indeed the very validity of the theory itself as a universal construct, since the United States is a preeminently modern society whose case the theory should cover—is severely limited.

Furthermore, the classic "demographic transition" does not seem to have happened in the United States, the demographic corollary of modernization which asserts that countries go through four stages of changing birth and death rates as they proceed from traditional to industrialized: death rates fall, while birth rates remain high, resulting in unprecedented population growth, and only after a time do birth rates drop to restore traditionally slow net growth and more stable population size. Transition theory may describe what happened in England in the eighteenth and nineteenth centuries, or (with revisions) in France, but it does not reflect the demographic history of North America.[19]

Many critiques of modernization are now in print and it is pointless to mention more than a few. Raymond Grew, in an essay entitled "Modernization and its Discontents,"[20] reminded his readers that the term "is vague as well as unat-

tractive, even offensive," has "serious built-in biases," is
unclear about its units of analysis, and has been seen, not
surprisingly, as "the political ideology of Western self-
interest." Nowadays it "evokes the distrust of a crew-cut; both
are seen as symbols of the fifties and sixties and of an optimistic American imperialism." In fact, Grew maintained,
there has never been a single theory of modernization but only
a lot of individual theories on often separate problems such as
families, workers, and cities. But despite its faults, he concluded, "a kind of common sense makes one hesitate to throw
the concept out. [It] can . . . help identify vital questions [al-
though] it provides no methods of its own . . . [and] its most
important findings in the future are likely to be about differences" among societies rather than similarities.[21]

Two other historians have recently pointed out, in different ways, that traditional and modern ways of life may coexist
in the same society or person, that they are not necessarily
sequential, that subcultural traditions may survive, adapted to
some extent, in a modernized society.[22] One, Thomas Bender,
urged a reemployment of Tönnies's *Gemeinschaft-Gesellschaft*
idea, but in its pristine form, which allowed the two to
coexist. Bender criticized Louis Wirth's well-known article on
"Urbanism as a Way of Life" (1937) as ahistorical, as positing
characteristics of urban society without allowing for how they
might change over time. According to Bender, Wirth suc-
cumbed to "a vision of unilinear and inevitable progress."
Modernization is simply "the foreign policy version of Wirth's
theory," formulated in the 1950s "to facilitate the 'development' of Third-World nations in ways that would avoid the
sort of political instability that might strengthen the Com-
munist World at the expense of the Free World." Bender pro-
ceeded to examine the historical nature of "community" in
America since the seventeenth century and built a "tentative
and speculative" time framework for understanding it. He cor-
rectly pointed out that over a dozen recent books have dis-

cussed the "logic of decay" of community in America, and hence obliquely modernization, but have confusingly dated it in the 1650s, 1690s, 1740s, 1780s, 1820s, 1850s, 1880s, and 1920s. He himself saw the years 1870 to 1920 as the central time when "social experience became bifurcated into what Tönnies called Gemeinschaft and Gesellschaft."[23]

This discussion of modernization theory suggests a frame for seeing how the United States does, and does not, fit into a transnational pattern. Modernization theory contains over-simplifications from a historical standpoint, especially in its unidirectional, progressive, dichotomous projections. A second problem, in the American case, is to what if any extent Americans have been "traditional." This must be solved by those who would apply modernization to American experience. Yet the historical record does not provide much evidence for traditional patterns in the sense used by Tönnies or Max Weber or the modernizers. America was never a "less-developed country." Nondeveloped surely, but not less- or under-developed. Although the seventeenth century (especially in New England) may have been a special case,[24] Americans were usually expansive, planners-ahead, money-makers, restless, "efficacious"[25] about their environment and its future. New England merchants and Chesapeake planters were deeply involved in the emerging transatlantic economy, and, in less dramatic ways, farmers and villagers were also involved in the marketplace and in small-scale agricultural entrepreneurship. American colonists in the eighteenth century had, as James Henretta wrote, an "aggressive psychological outlook which most clearly differentiated the inhabitants of eighteenth century America from a traditional peasantry."[26]

Not every American, all the time and everywhere, shared these modern traits, but then, not all do today. The point is that modern traits were present early and often. In 1836 a report to the New York State Medical Society fretted that "The population of the United States is beyond that of other countries an anxious one . . . we are an anxious, care-worn people."[27] Michel Chevalier, that great French liberal of the nineteenth century, visited the United States in the early 1830s and noticed how businesslike everybody was. In Cincinnati, "Public opinion is on the lookout to banish any habits of dissipation, however innocent, that might get a footing in society, and make a life of leisure tolerable." In New York City, "Nothing . . . is more melancholy than the seventh day . . . after such a Sunday, the labour of Monday is a delightful pastime."[28] Chevalier's more famous touring compatriot, Alexis de Tocqueville, found much the same thing:

> An American, instead of going in a leisure hour to dance merrily at some place of public resort, as the fellows of his calling continue to do throughout the greater part of Europe, shuts himself up at home to drink. He thus enjoys two pleasures: he can go on thinking of his business, and he can get drunk decently by his own fireside.

And, unlike European peasants,

> Almost all the farmers of the United States combine some trade with agriculture; most of them make agriculture itself a trade. It seldom happens that an American farmer settles for good upon the land which he occupies . . . [but] brings land into tillage in order to sell it again.[29]

Tocqueville exaggerated somewhat; some farmers, especially older ones, did put down roots. American workers resisted the work ethic from Franklin's time to the present, to various degrees,[30] and farmers only gradually shifted from semisubsistence production to production largely for markets.[31]

The traditional-modern patterns were (and are) seldom exclusive of each other. But compared to European peasantries[32] Americans were modern at least as early as the first half of the eighteenth century. We could write this off to Anglo-Saxon moneygrubbing or to the Protestant work ethic or to some other myth, but the traits of modernity also characterized

Germans, Swedes, Irish, and later immigrants. As Marcus Hansen, the pioneering historian of immigration, put it, "They were Americans before they landed." The same was definitely true of Poles and southern Italians who began arriving in the United States in some numbers in the 1880s: they were truly migrant workers, responding to marginal differences in a transatlantic labor market in order to improve their situations as entrepreneurs or landowners at home.[33]

Classic social theory, and specific theories of modernization derived from it, will not apply strictly to the American historical experience. This is not to say that Americans failed to "modernize" in some sense. Agriculture changed in the nineteenth and twentieth centuries, traditional and modern traits intermingled in subcultures and in the general culture, and of course beyond those facts is the more general truth that social structures like those suggested by "traditional" or "modern" do not hold still over long time periods. Sociological terms may be argued as if they were static, but the realities they represent are not. All social realities change over time, though some change very slowly.[34] So it was in America. But from early times, America evidenced modernity, sharing in England's already-begun modernization of the eighteenth century,[35] being not so much the "first new nation" as the first nation that was never old. The concept of modernization thus has some suggestive or heuristic value for students of American social history. But it is certainly not faultless or exhaustive.

A very different explanation of social change is the frontier thesis of Frederick Jackson Turner. Rather than revolving about transnational and universal processes like modernization, it stresses the uniqueness of American development. The frontier thesis fits the pre-1890 American experience rather well, and though it stops at that point, it has with some justice been called the only comprehensive explanation of American history that anyone has yet devised. Historians are familiar with it, but it will do no harm to quote a few passages from Turner's paper of 1893, "The Significance of the Frontier in American History," his fullest enunciation of his frontier thesis.

"The existence of an area of free land," he declared, "its continuous recession, and the advance of American settlement westward, explain American development." A sweeping statement. Furthermore, the frontier, that area of free land, was pushed westward and was transformed into a civilized region by a continuing, repeating social process:

> The United States lies like a huge page in the history of society. Line by line as we read this continental page from West to East we find the record of social evolution. It begins with the Indian and the hunter; it goes on to tell of the disintegration of savagery by the entrance of the trader, the pathfinder of civilization; we read the annals of the pastoral stage in ranch life; the exploita-tion of the soil by the raising of unrotated crops of corn and wheat in sparsely settled farming communities; the intensive culture of the denser farm settlement; and finally the manufactur-ing organization with city and factory system. This page is famil-iar to the student of census statistics, but how little of it has been used by our historians. Particularly in eastern states this page is a palimpsest.

Further, "The growth of nationalism and the evolution of American political institutions were dependent on the advance of the frontier." And it was

> to the frontier [that] the American intellect owes its striking characteristics. That coarseness and strength combined with acuteness and acquisitiveness; that practical, inventive turn of mind, quick to find expedients; that masterful grasp of material things, lacking in the artistic but powerful to effect great ends; that restless, nervous energy; that dominant individualism, working for good and for evil, and withal that buoyancy and exuberance which comes with freedom—these are traits of the frontier, or traits called out elsewhere because of the existence of the frontier.

Turner was struck by the statement in the report prefacing the

federal census of 1890 that a continuous frontier line had
ceased to exist during the 1880s. Pockets of land remained
empty, but for the first time, a line from Canada to Mexico,
west of which was virtually unsettled land, there for the taking, could no longer be drawn on the map. Since Columbus
first sailed, Turner reminded his listerners, "America has been
another name for opportunity . . . [and] movement has been
its dominant fact." But in 1893, "four centuries from the dis-
covery of America, at the end of a hundred years of life under
the Constitution, the frontier has gone, and with its going has
closed the first period of American history."[36]

That is the nub of the Turner thesis. It has had many crit-
ics, not least because Turner seemed to overargue the role of
the frontier in shaping American personality, to underargue
urban and industrial history and class conflict, and to attribute
to the influence of the frontier too many social and personal
qualities (though these were by no means all flattering or
romanticized). But these and other criticisms aside, does
Turner still have anything to tell us? I think he does, and I
think he might have told us more had he lived into our own
time and been able to see more clearly how the frontier became significant in an even longer time span and larger context
than he realized, either in 1893 or by the time he died in 1932.
In any case, it is obviously true, *grosso modo*, that the existence
of a very large virgin wilderness, accessible (the more so after
the building of the railroads), inexpensive, and easily
exploited, was a uniquely important difference between American development and that of other First World countries in the
eighteenth and nineteenth centuries, and of "less-developed"
countries in the twentieth, possibly excepting Brazil. Though
the role of the frontier in American history has been exten-
sively evaluated, more can be said, and the point about available land reapplied. Also, the frontier idea reflects on modernization theory: although it is a kind of modernization scheme
of its own, the frontier idea is particular to America while

modernization theory, in its classic formulations, is transnational and transtemporal. Yet if we understand both ideas broadly, they may complement each other.

Modernization theorists have stressed increased control over the environment, the "efficacy factor," as a mark of modernization. They associate efficacy with the break from traditional peasant or rural ways and the entry into urban life, mass politics, and other modern behavior. But if the essence of this process is the presence of efficacy rather than the place where it was exercised, then we can find it not only in the rural-to-urban movement on which modernizationists focus so often, but also in the rural-to-rural movement, the rapid expansion, the aggressive exploitation of land and resources typical of the United States in the eighteenth and nineteenth centuries. Another point: education is a key to modernization, according to its theorists. If we concede that education can take place outside of classrooms, laboratories, or libraries, all of which were strikingly absent from American frontier regions, then possibly the United States might yet squeeze under the modernization umbrella. As William Appleman Williams once wrote, the frontier as an exploitable area was an educator, not the least of whose lessons was expansionism. In America it did not teach peasant ways, but entrepreneurial ones. "The frontier in some ways took the place of formal education," according to Williams; "a kind of non-intellectual learning by surviving and succeeding became part of the American attitude at an early date."[37]

The frontier also had much to do with the early establishment and continued predominance of property owning or property seeking among Americans. Marx and Engels thought that class struggle could not break out in the United States until "undeveloped social conditions" and easy ownership of land had ceased. Engels wrote in 1886 that in America, "every one could become, if not a capitalist, at all events an independent man, producing or trading, with his own means, for his

should be familiar. "I think I may fairly make two postulata,"
Malthus began.

> First, that food is necessary to the existence of man.
> Secondly, that the passion between the sexes is necessary,
> and will remain nearly in its present state.
> These two laws ever since we have had any knowledge of
> mankind, appear to have been fixed laws of our nature, [and we
> can expect no change] . . . without an immediate act of power in
> that Being who first arranged the system of the universe; and for
> the advantage of his creatures, still executes, according to fixed
> laws, all its various operations.

On these two observations Malthus rested his grim and famous conclusion:

> Assuming, then, my postulata as granted, I say, that the power
> of population is indefinitely greater than the power in the earth
> to produce subsistence for man. Population, when unchecked,
> increases in a geometrical ratio. Subsistence increases only in an
> arithmetical ratio. A slight acquaintance with numbers will shew
> the immensity of the first power in comparison of the second.[44]

Malthus's entry in the *Dictionary of National Biography* was
written by no less eminent a Victorian than Leslie Stephen,
who assured us that Malthus was "a singularly amiable
man."[45] But Malthus, the graduate of the mathematics tripos,
could not shrink from a Q.E.D.: the great disparity between
geometrical population growth and arithmetical subsistence
growth argued conclusively

> against the perfectibility of the mass of mankind. . . . And, that
> the superior power of population cannot be checked without
> producing misery or vice, the ample portion of these two bitter
> ingredients in the cup of human life, and the continuance of the
> physical causes that seem to have produced them, bear too con-
> vincing a testimony.[46]

In the second and expanded edition of the *Essay*, which
Malthus brought out in 1803, he urged another alternative

besides vice and misery, the voluntary one of "moral restraint," by which he meant delaying marriage (and staying
celibate before marriage), thereby reducing the number of
births. This offered some hope for progress and human im-
provement, though that was by no means certain.[47]

Malthus at one point considered whether emigration
might be an "adequate remedy" to overpopulation, but he did
not think much of it. "When we revert to experience, and to
the actual state of the uncivilized parts of the globe . . . it will
appear but a very weak palliative." To support this view he
recited several disastrous attempts to colonize in the New
World, efforts that led to famine and death, as in early Virginia, New England, and "the Barbadoes."[48] Nassau Senior,
an English economist of the next generation, criticized
Malthus in the 1840s for disregarding emigration as a check on
population. Senior, like many English thinkers and doers
(though not enough of them), was concerned about Ireland
and its overpopulation, and declared emigration to be the only
remedy. He made the interesting observation that while populations for whom property holding is easy—the Americans of
the eighteenth or nineteenth century, for whom land was
abundant—have high birth rates, it is paradoxically true that
poverty, verging on destitution, leads also to high birth rates,
as in Ireland: ". . . when men are so indigent that they cannot
become poorer, and so abject that they cannot be more de-
graded, they naturally seize whatever pleasures are within
their reach without caring for the consequences."[49]

Malthus did, however, allow for certain prosperous colonies to provide a solution to threats of overpopulation. Ever
since the time of the classical Greeks, colonies occasionally
provided an escape from the vice and misery that inevitably
overtook populations that outdistanced their food supplies.
Malthus called such places "a plenty of rich land to be had for
little or nothing," and in another place, "a great plenty of fer-
tile uncultivated land."[50] Such words described the former

English colonies in North America, as they had developed in the eighteenth century, and Malthus was very much aware of that. Citing Ezra Stiles of Connecticut and other eighteenth-century American observers, Malthus graciously concluded,

> In the United States of America, where the means of subsistence have been more ample, the manners of the people more pure, and consequently the checks to early marriage fewer, than in any of the modern states of Europe, the population has been found to double itself in twenty-five years. This ratio of increase, though short of the utmost power of population, yet as the result of actual experience, we will take as our rule; and say,
>   That population, when unchecked, goes on doubling itself every twenty-five years, or increases in a geometrical ratio.[51]

In fact, he pointed out, back-country areas doubled in only fifteen years in America.[52] But he took a conservative twenty-five as his average, and it became the famous "Malthusian ratio," the natural, unchecked rate of increase of human populations when the means of subsistence are plentiful.

Presently available data for the eighteenth century are much the same as Malthus's and have not improved enough to upset his figures. If a population grows at a rate of 3 percent per year, it will double in just under twenty-five years. American population in the eighteenth century increased in some areas at 4 percent, doubling in nineteen years, or even 5 percent, doubling in fifteen years. Rates above 3 percent were true in the nineteenth century of Americans, of both English and French Canadians in the St. Lawrence Valley,[53] and even of Sioux Indians on the northern Great Plains.[54] When would this staggering growth stop? Malthus knew:

> Even civil liberty, all powerful as it is, will not create fresh land. The Americans may be said, perhaps, to enjoy a greater degree of civil liberty, now they are an independent people, than while they were in subjection to England; but we may be perfectly sure, that population will not long continue to increase with the same rapidity as it did then.[55]

Yet an English traveler who published his impressions in 1821 wrote, "Mr Malthus would not be understood here."[56] In fact, Americans were able to ignore Malthus, to continue to increase almost as rapidly, for several more decades. More precisely, they were able to multiply in their "new habitat," which Malthus clearly understood was very different from Europe in a demographic sense.

Malthus made a great contribution. As Australian political economist Ian Bowen put it, Malthus "once and for all [drew] mankind's attention to the fact that there were limits to expansion. Once the postulate is granted that food . . . cannot be indefinitely expanded, then it follows that population cannot be indefinitely increased."[57] In the process of stating his population theory, Malthus became the chief founder of modern demographic theory and historical demography. Not that no one before him had remarked on population. Many had.[58] But no one clarified for English readers, as Malthus did, questions about fertility, mortality, migration, income, resources, and class—the stuff of sociology, economics, and much of history. After the population essay and other works, it was possible for Malthus's friend and critic, David Ricardo, to marry population and economics,[59] for Nassau Senior to revise the theory to apply to Ireland and to account for population growth among the destitute, and for later scholars to continue working on the research agenda that Malthus had explored. Malthus himself wrote that we know too little about the oscillations between times of plenty and times of misery, because "the histories of mankind that we possess are histories only of the higher classes."[60] As for whether America was unique, Malthus as a student of population knew that it was a "new habitat," but he expected that it would become more and more like Europe as land became less available, the means of subsistence less abundant, and population growth less rapid. The story became more complicated than that, but, like modernization theory and Turner's frontier, Malthus (and Ricardo and Senior) advanced the understanding of America in both its uniqueness and its transnational context.

Structures and Conjunctures: The French Connection

Malthus's call for histories of all classes, not just the elites, was not really heeded by any large group of professional historians until Marc Bloch and Lucien Febvre founded the journal *Annales d'histoire sociale et économique* in Strasbourg in 1929, and when they and others coalesced into the *"Annales* school,"* centered in Paris after World War II.[61] *Annales* history encompasses more than demographic history, but has helped it flourish in France and Britain. Demographic history, hardly thought of in the United States before 1965, since developed after that into a substantial body of scholarly literature.[62] To a few historians before then, the importance of a history of population, in itself and for other histories, was not in doubt. Turner, in notes for a lecture delivered in 1923, refers to census data and to prominent demographers, and to Malthus. Population was a concern of Turner's, as were the "Nordic alarmists" of that time, neo-Malthusians who feared that population in the United States and the world would outrun food supplies, minerals, petroleum, and other necessities within a generation or two. Turner's frontier observation of 1893 was itself demographic and geographic.[63] Nearly ninety years later, an American demographic historian pleaded for more studies meeting "the historical demographer's ideal . . . informed speculation and models for explanation, a knowledge of demographic methods and comparative findings, and hard work in the sources."[64] At about the same time, Robert Parke, of the Social Science Research Council, cited areas where policy makers should take better account of demographic studies; very regrettably he omitted historical work.[65]

European authorities on the importance of population in history include England's H. J. Habakkuk, who said in 1958 that for those who care for the overmastering pattern, the elements are evidently there for a heroically simplified version of English history before the nineteenth century, in which the long-term movements in prices, in income distribution, in investment, in real wages and in migration are dominated by changes in the growth of population.[66]

Similarly, Fernand Braudel of the *Annalistes*, in his masterpiece *The Mediterranean and the Mediterranean World in the Age of Philip II*, reflecting on the doubling of population around the Mediterranean between 1500 and 1600, wrote,

> . . . this biological revolution was the major factor in all the other revolutions with which we are concerned, more important than the Turkish conquest, the discovery and colonization of America, or the imperial vocation of Spain. Had it not been for the increase in the numbers of men, would any of these glorious chapters ever have been written?[67]

Other prominent witnesses abound who will testify that population is important in history, that it should be "the starting point for constructing an *histoire totale*,"[68] and that Americans have not absorbed it well enough into their thinking about the past.

Embedded in Braudel's book is an ingenious scheme for looking at history and relating passing events and longer-run patterns. His terms should clarify what I want to say about the periodization of American history based on population changes. In *The Mediterranean* and other of his writings, Braudel seeks to isolate immediate, concrete events, the *événementielle*, as surface happenings on more lasting units of time, periods of twelve to fifty years, which he calls *conjonctures*. These in turn rest on much longer-lasting *structures*. Events are short-run (*courte durée*), *conjonctures* are middle-run (*moyenne durée*), and *structures* are long-run (*longue durée*). Everything changes. Nothing in human society is absolutely static over time. But *longue durée* patterns may change very slowly, lasting with little measurable change for centuries.[69]

The challenge which Braudel throws at historians is to identify the *moyenne* and *longue durées* out of the chaos of passing events. In what follows, the entities I call the frontier-rural mode and the metropolitan mode are akin to Braudel's *structures*. I use the word "mode" because it is less ambiguous than the cognate English word "structure" for *structure*, but I still mean a set of long-lasting social (and therefore economic and cultural) patterns, changing slowly over ten or twenty decades, shaping the lives and behavior of the great majority of people who lived in that place in that period. "Mode" means *structure*, and period, as when I say "frontier-rural period," means the span of time when that mode was prevalent. "Conjuncture," as I will use it, refers to the briefer time when two modes coexisted and interacted.[70]

A Demographic Observation: Growth Rate Plateaus

At one point in his book, Braudel was writing about violence, poverty, brigandage, and piracy in Italy and Germany in the sixteenth century. This provoked the thought that the terrorism of the 1970s in those countries—the work of the Baader-Meinhof gang, the P.L.O. at the Munich Olympics in 1972, the Red Brigades who killed Aldo Moro, the kneecappers, and others—may be explainable in part by long-term historical structures of those areas. Braudel's point was more philosophical, however; out of a series of instances of violence he reflects on the task of historians. "Are these incidents," he asks,

> trivial happenings in themselves, the surface signs of a valid social history? . . . . Is this evidence meaningful at some deeper level? That is the historian's problem. To answer yes, as I intend to do, means being willing to see correlations, regular patterns and general trends where at first sight there appear only incoherence, anarchy, a series of unrelated happenings.[71]

With this mandate (and keeping in mind the useful ideas on

social change provided by the modernization theorists, Turner, and Malthus) we now seek "regular patterns and general trends" in the history of the American population. I offer an observation which is simple and concrete, but which has not been remarked upon as far as I know. It divides American history into periods on the basis of mass population data and may therefore help solve such questions as when Americans modernized, if ever; where the frontier ended and what it meant; even where the balance of population and resources may go in the near and middle future.

Total figures of the United States population exist for ten-year intervals back to 1790, thanks to the Census, and well back into the colonial seventeenth century, thanks to historians. These figures are reliable within the reasonable limits demanded for comparing the speed of population growth. When the increases in each decade are translated into percents, and are graphed, three distinct plateaus appear (see table 1 and figure 1).[72] Wild fluctuations occur before 1670, when the colonial population was less than 100,000, or before 1700, when it reached 250,000. Before those dates the sparseness of people made the seventeenth century into a sort of statistical *Vorzeit*, or prehistory.[73] From (very roughly) 1720 until just after 1860, population in America increased at exceedingly rapid rates. This period, from the early eighteenth century until the early 1860s, may be considered, from a demographic standpoint, to be the first phase of American history.

From the 1670s through the 1850s, a period during which the total population rose from 112,000 to 31,443,000, the average rate of growth per decade was 34.6 percent. The rate fluctuated within a wide range in the early decades when population was small, between a low 19.5 percent in the 1690s to a high 41.3 percent in the 1780s. But after 1790, with the population at about 4 million and rising, the fluctuations fell within the high but narrow range of 33 to 36 percent, averag-

TABLE I

Population of the United States, 1630–1980

Year	A: total population (in thousands)[1]	B: percent increase in preceding decade[2]	C: percent rural[3]
1630	4.6	—	
1640	27	487.0	
1650	50	85.2	
1660	75	50.0	
1670	112	49.3	
1680	152	35.7	
1690	210	38.2	
1700	251	19.5	
1710	332	32.3	
1720	466	40.4	
1730	629	35.0	
1740	906	44.0	
1750	1,171	29.2	
1760	1,594	36.1	
1770	2,148	34.8	
1780	2,780	29.4	
1790	3,929	41.3	95
1800	5,308	35.1	94
1810	7,240	36.4	93
1820	9,638	33.1	93
1830	12,866	33.5	91
1840	17,069	32.7	89
1850	23,192	35.9	85
1860	31,443	35.6	80
1870	39,818	26.6	75
1880	50,156	26.0	72
1890	62,948	25.5	65
1900	75,995	20.7	60
1910	91,972	21.0	54
1920	105,771	14.9	49
1930	122,775	16.1	44
1940	131,669	7.2	43

1950	150,697	14.5	36
1960	179,323	19.0	30
1970	203,235	13.3	26
1980	221,500	9.0	

[1]Source: *Historical Statistics* 1975, series Z1-Z19, A2. 1980 approximate, from Census report P-25, no. 881.
[2]Source: Computed from column A.
[3]Source: *Historical Statistics* 1975, series A203. "Rural" means the proportion living on farms or in villages smaller than 2,500 (after 1940, not including suburban fringes, which have been counted as "urban").

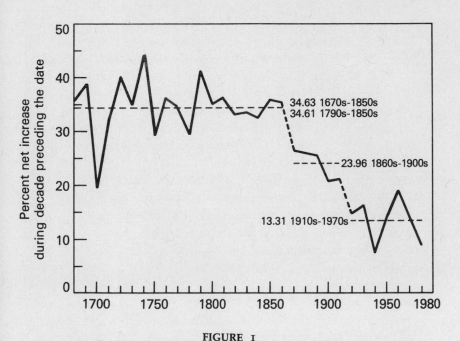

FIGURE 1

The three plateaus: Rates of
population growth, by decade

ing 34.6 percent from the 1790s through the 1850s. That rate of growth was slightly higher than the Malthusian ratio. The American population doubled about every twenty-two years. But no Malthusian disaster happened. Famine and pestilence did not sweep the land. Epidemics of yellow fever, cholera, and smallpox hardly made a dent except among Indians. Wars were few and relatively local.[74] Sufficient food and land were available to satisfy physical and economic cravings, and to encourage rapid expansion of territory and population.

As the land area of the United States was extended to include the trans-Appalachian West by the Treaty of Paris of 1783, ending the Revolutionary War, and then into the immense regions of Louisiana in 1803, the Floridas by 1819, Texas in 1845, Oregon in 1846, and the Southwest in 1848, the density of the population barely doubled while the numbers of population doubled and redoubled and re-redoubled in an exuberant drive to fill these regions productively with Anglo-Americans. The extremely rapid growth, although it involved tens of millions of individual people, had certain features that were practically constant. Although we are employing aggregate data from censuses, aggregates which flatten out a wide range of individual behavior by the averaging and collecting process, nonetheless we can make some valid general statements. The expanding population was rural, (see table 2) and its expansion rarely involved town-building except as supply centers and jumping-off points into exploitable rural areas were demanded.[75] Expansion sprang from high birth rates rather than dropping death rates, or from heavy net migration, at least until the late 1840s. The areas growing most rapidly in population were those just behind the frontier, areas of six to forty-five people per square mile:[76] not the rawest frontier, or the more settled areas, but areas with enough cultivation and available land to permit new families to form and to build farms. The long period from the early eighteenth century to about 1860, with its very rapid (and, after 1790, very steady) growth, deserves to be called the frontier-rural period in American history.

In the 1860s, the rate of population growth suddenly dropped. From the customary increase of over 35 percent in the 1850s, the increase in the 1860s fell to just over 26 percent. It remained at about that level through the 1870s and 1880s. It fell again in the 1890s and from 1900 to 1910, but not as steeply, to about 21 percent. During the half century from the early 1860s to about 1915, growth per decade averaged 24 percent, or about a third slower than the growth rate prevailing for more than a century and a half before then. A distinct and sudden change had taken place around 1860, signaling a new period in demographic and social history. It was a bi-level period, lasting about fifty years, and, for reasons to be seen, it can be called the Great Conjuncture.

After 1915, population never again grew as much as 20 percent in a decade.[77] The census of 1920 placed the total population at 15 percent higher than 1910. From 1920 until the beginning of the 1980s, increases have averaged 13 percent, ranging from a high of 18 during the baby-boom years of the 1950s to lows of 7 or 8 percent during the depression-ridden 1930s and the 1970s. Thus the years from just before 1920 to the early 1980s—and perhaps well beyond—form a third phase in American history. The first period consisted of growth in the frontier-rural mode almost exclusively. The third has seen virtually no frontier-rural growth, but almost purely a metropolitan mode, involving industry, interregional trade and business organization, urbanization, and suburbanization. Agricultural population has stabilized in absolute numbers, or fallen, while urban population has continued to eat into the total at a rate of about 5 percent per decade (as has happened since the 1840s). Almost four out of five Americans lived in urban areas by 1980—and practically all the rest were touched by metropolitan life via the media and the marketplace, even though some were moving away from the physical,

TABLE 2
Rural and urban population growth, and rural as a proportion of total U.S. growth, by decade, 1790s–1960s

Decade ending	A. Rural % increase	B. Urban % increase	C. % of total growth acc'ted for by rural
1800	33.7	59.4	96.0
1810	34.7	63.0	95.3
1820	33.2	32.0	100.3
1830	31.2	62.6	93.1
1840	29.7	63.7	90.8
1850	29.1	92.1	81.1
1860	28.4	75.4	78.1
avg. 1790s–1850s	31.4	64.0	90.7
1870	13.6	59.3	51.1
1880	25.7	42.7	98.8
1890	13.4	56.4	52.5
1900	12.2	36.4	58.9
1910	9.0	39.3	42.9
avg. 1860s–1900s	14.8	46.8	60.8
1920	3.2	29.0	21.5
1930	4.4	27.3	27.3
1940	6.4	7.9	88.9
1950*	7.9/−5.2	19.5/29.6	54.5/−35.9
1960	−0.9	29.9	−4.7
1970	+0.2	19.2	−0.2
avg. 1910s–1960s	2.7	22.7	27.2

Column C is arrived at by dividing percent rural increase (column A above) by percent total increase (column B of table 1—not by column B above).

Rate of rural increase declines. So does rate of urban increase. But rural increase accounts for more than half of the total U.S. increase until almost 1920.

Sources: *Historical Statistics* 1975. Column A, series A69;

geographic metropolises. But few could escape the mode. Urban growth has always been slower than rural growth in the United States, and the decline in the rate of growth through most of American history forms two parallel lines, the urban below the rural.[78]

As the metropolitan mode became established in the middle and late nineteenth century and then became predominant after 1915 or so, population growth was typically much slower than during the frontier-rural and Conjuncture periods, in spite of boom towns of the recent past like Los Angeles and Houston, in spite of the exodus of blacks from the South to northern and midwestern cities between 1915 and 1970, and in spite of the emergence of a suburban-dwelling majority. Metropolitan growth differs from frontier-rural not only in its slowness but also in its causes, outcomes, and economic and demographic character.

From 35 percent per decade in the first period, to 24 percent in the second, to below 14 in the third: that is the regular pattern for nearly three hundred years. The regularity is admittedly less stark if we leave aside net migration from Europe, Africa, and Asia, as Malthus did, and deal only with the natural increase from the surplus of births over deaths in the existing population. Without immigration the step-wise pattern of downward plateaus of growth rates is a little less clear. But it is only slightly blurred, not fully eroded by any means. And certainly immigration cannot be left out of any general treatment of the American experience without violating the story irreparably.[79]

A leading demographic historian reviewed the state of his field in 1979, noted as have others that much good work has been done since the mid-1960s, but lamented that "there is no

---

column B, series A57; column C, series A69 divided by series A2.
*Census definition of "urban" changes. This decade is omitted in calculating averages of 1910s–1960s.

consensus on periodization, and 'linear' notions of every sort are now questioned."[80] One can add that much of that work is specialized, and attempts at comprehensive histories are rumored but not published. The three-phase periodization, based on plateaus of growth, may be helpful in this regard. The question arises as to why the decline in growth was steplike rather than steady, and I will not answer that to a demographer's satisfaction. But it evidently happened, and in succeeding chapters I will describe the modes and conjuncture that the plateaus represent. Components of change, including decline in the rural growth rate, decline in the urban growth rate, the relation between the two, the baby-boom anomaly, changes in mortality rates and in migration patterns, and other aspects of demographic history, have been remarked upon and continue to be studied. Enough is now understood, I believe, to permit a comprehensive look, even if it is tentative. What is offered here, then, is a framework for social history based on a demographic observation involving the American population throughout its history. The framework might well accommodate many other elements—politics, economics, *mentalités*[81] —but on this occasion they appear, if at all, as suggested byroads.

Frederick Jackson Turner might have seen the three-stage pattern of growth rates had he lived into our own day, conscious as he was of demographic patterns and graphic techniques.[82] But he died in March 1932, before the pattern became clear. He might have seen that American history did not divide into two periods, frontier and postfrontier, but into three: frontier-rural, metropolitan, and the conjuncture of the two modes to form a period in between. He did see that the existence of a vast mass of readily available land was a fact of cardinal importance for a long time, as no one considering American history can seriously deny, though many have given it too little weight. Turner called attention to the frontier in 1893. In 1923 he warned of the "likelihood that we in New

England and the Midwest in general will not appreciate the importance of the rural factor in our history and in the problems of the future."[83] In the 1980s we may run that risk, immersed in the metropolitan *mentalité* as we are, and we should remind ourselves that the rural past is not dead, or, as Faulkner said, is not even past.

Turner was conscious that the frontier did not end "with a bang" in 1890, as he once put it, that 1880–1900 formed some kind of transition phase which had not fully ended until the early twentieth century, that homestead patents were still being issued in 1920. But the Census of 1920, with its evidence of rising farm tenancy, depressed him, and he worried that population pressure and rising costs of farmland would create an American peasantry for the first time. He was well aware of changes in agriculture during the eighteenth and nineteenth centuries, and at one point (in 1926) declared that "frontier advance . . . went on until not only the frontier *line*, as mapped by Henry Gannett [of the Census] could no longer be depicted, but until the frontier *phase* of our history drew to its close." And he dated that phase from Bacon's Rebellion (1676) to La Follette's presidential candidacy (1924)—dates based on nondemographic events but which mark the limits of the frontier-rural mode very closely to the rates-of-growth pattern.[84] In his final days, however, Turner did not clearly see that new forms of opportunity, especially white-collar jobs, had begun to replace the lost opportunities of frontiers, and that the metropolitan mode had arrived, bringing new ways of living which were not deserving of the pessimism with which he, and more alarmist observers of the 1920s, regarded it. The end of the frontier was not the end of America, and by the time Turner died, the transitional phase was already past.[85]

The most interesting part of our observation about growth rates is the emergence of a transition phase of about fifty years, with the end of the frontier line falling almost exactly at the midpoint of that phase. Instead of a simple, dichotomous

shift from frontier to postfrontier, or from traditional to modern, or (most popularly and oversimply) from rural to urban,
we find rapid frontier-rural growth continuing after 1890 and
through much of the Conjuncture, and at the same time the
spread of metropolitan growth, especially in the northeastern
quarter of the country. In the final years of the Conjuncture,
frontier-rural growth breathed its last, giving up the field before 1920 to exclusively metropolitan patterns of life. Because
both modes operated between the 1860s and about 1915,
those years deserve the name "Great Conjuncture." The crucial
point is that the newer form of growth was not simply replac-
ing the older. Both happened at once in those years.

Through much of their population history, Americans ignored Malthus. They exhibited hardly any sign until well into
the twentieth century of the "moral restraint" he preached, but
on the other hand they suffered little of the "vice and misery"
of which he warned.

II

From Prehistory to the Frontier-Rural Mode, 1500–1720

This chapter treats of the European demographic matrix from which colonies sprang in the sixteenth and seventeenth centuries, and the impact of colonization on aboriginal Americans; of the social-demographic nature of English colonies in New England and astride the Chesapeake in the seventeenth century, a period I term *Vorzeit;* and of the emergence of the frontier-rural mode in the early eighteenth century. The dates 1500 and 1720 are approximate, and indicate general trends rather than precisely datable events.

Old World to New World in the Sixteenth Century

We begin in western Europe and surrounding waters in about 1500. A cycle of population expansion had begun in the late fifteenth century and was to continue through the sixteenth. The bubonic plague that had scourged Europe from the 1340s into the fifteenth century was mostly dormant and would not reappear widely until the seventeenth century. Harvests were generally good, markets reasonably efficient in bringing food to cities. For these and other reasons, not all of

35

them well understood as yet, the population of Europe rose from perhaps 70 million to over 100 million in the sixteenth century. In the Mediterranean countries it may have doubled between 1530 and 1590.[1] In many respects sixteenth-century Europe remained medieval. The Mediterranean was a world to itself, taking sixty days to cross just as it had in Roman times, and remained "the centre of the world, a strong and brilliant universe . . . for a hundred years after Christopher Columbus and Vasco da Gama."[2] Still, the brilliant universe was beginning to shed its light in new places. In the sixteenth century the Spanish and Portuguese established their vast empires in North and South America. The French began to create one only slightly smaller, an empire ultimately stretching from the Caribbean and the mouth of the Mississippi northeastward to the Great Lakes and the Gulf of St. Lawrence, almost the entire eastern two-thirds of North America.[3]

These empires, however, did not swarm with Europeans, because Europe could not yet provide them. The startling thing is not how many people left Europe, but how few. The early parties that went to Mexico and Peru numbered in the hundreds, and they confronted an indigenous population numbering in the millions. In all of the Americas in 1500 somewhere between 50 million and 100 million native people lived, the great majority of them in the coastal or Andean mountain regions from the Tropic of Cancer southward to below the Tropic of Capricorn.[4] With amazing speed and ease, the few hundred Spaniards conquered the Mexican and Peruvian Indians, who outnumbered them more than one hundred thousand to one. How was it possible? The Spanish did have horses and gunpowder, which were formidable advantages, but not enough to account for their victory after the initial shock was past. The Spanish, however, also had the silent and terrible weapon of European contagious diseases. As happened to the peoples of Europe when plague struck in the fourteenth century, the Indians of Mexico and Peru were dev-

astated by exposure to diseases for which they had no internal
immunity whatsoever, genetic or otherwise.

By 1500, western Europe "had much to give and little to
receive in the way of new human infections."[5] It gave much to
the native inhabitants of Central and South America. Smallpox
ravaged central and coastal Mexico in 1522, killing millions.
From then on, smallpox, together with diseases mild to a
European (measles, chicken pox, whooping cough), or more
serious (malaria and influenza), or carried by African slaves of
Europeans (yellow fever, which appeared in the seventeenth
century), wiped out most of the native peoples. The population of Mexico, probably over 25 million when Cortez arrived
in 1519, plunged hideously. By 1568 it numbered no more
than 3 million. Another epidemic in 1576–77 cut it in half,
and by 1605 only about a million were alive. Moreover, European diseases more often struck down young adults than the
aged or the children. The ancient gods were silent. Indian society fell apart, famine followed epidemic, and "a demographic disaster with no known parallel in human history"
was complete.[6]

To the north, in what became the United States and
Canada, no such destruction took place; tropical and Mediterranean diseases made less headway, and far fewer Indians
lived there.[7] The "decimation factor"—the ratio of Indian
population at its pre-Columbian height compared to its lowest
point thereafter—may have been 25 to 1 in coastal-tropical
Mexico, but 10 to 1 in most of the future United States and 5
to 1 in future Canada.[8] Colder climate and, more importantly,
a more primitive and nomadic culture scattered over large
areas allowed Indians farther north to avoid epidemics with a
little more success than did the Inca, the Aztecs, and other
densely populated cultures. A recent and cautious estimate put
the Indian population of the future United States and Canada
at about 2.2 million in 1500.[9] In 1600 the density of native
population never exceeded ten persons per square mile and

was much less in most areas.[10] The Iroquois Confederacy,
which caused so much difficulty in fact (and provided so much
material for fiction) in the French and Indian War of 1754–63,
almost surely never exceeded 17,000 people spread over hundreds of square miles. The Powhatans, who except for
Pocahontas gave the early settlers in Virginia much grief,
numbered perhaps 9,000.[11] The removals in the 1830s of the
"civilized tribes" from Georgia, Florida, and adjacent states to
present-day Arkansas and Oklahoma affected about a hundred
thousand Indians, a very large group of people but few compared to the 3.5 million whites in the South Atlantic states at
that time.[12] Everywhere, the Indians' contact with European-
Americans, and with Africans, brought demographic disaster,
from smallpox and other contagious diseases, from wars with
the colonists, and from wars among themselves.

Warring among tribes had gone on long before Europeans
arrived, although wars with the Europeans and their descendants have received greater attention, at the time and since.
But the worst killer of Indians was the series of epidemics that
struck them down from the seventeenth through the
nineteenth centuries, across time and across the continent.[13]
Peter Kalm, sent by the Swedish Academy of Science in 1748
to observe and report on American conditions, wrote that the
Indian population had been thinning out since the late seventeenth century. Some supposedly sold their lands and went
west,

> But in reality . . . most of them ended their days before, either
> by wars among themselves, or by the small-pox, a disease which
> the Indians were unacquainted with before their commerce with
> the Europeans, and which since that time has killed incredible
> numbers of them. For . . . they do not understand fever or other
> internal diseases.[14]

Ezra Stiles of Connecticut, writing in 1783, believed that there
were no more than 40,000 Indians east of the Mississippi and

north of the Ohio by that time, and Thomas Jefferson, in his *Notes on Virginia* of 1782, attributed the decline in Indian population to "spirituous liquors, the small-pox, war, and an abridgement of territory."[15] While the colonists of European stock were ravaged by smallpox, yellow fever, malaria, cholera, and other diseases (though never the plague) in the eighteenth and much of the nineteenth centuries, the native population suffered far worse. The curious thing, in the long run of American history, is not that the English and later the Americans consistently defeated the Indians, but that they had so much trouble doing it, considering the incidence of debility, demoralization, and death resulting from European and African diseases, which reduced the Indians' already small numbers and drained them of resilience and spirit even when they lived.

Vorzeit *in English America: The Seventeenth Century*

Europe's tentative entry into the modern pattern of population growth in the sixteenth century stalled in the seventeenth. England and Holland grew but slowly, France hardly at all. The great age of the Baroque, of Louis XIV, and the Glorious Revolution it may have been, but in demographic terms it was gloomy, stagnant, and long. Death visited more frequently than in the centuries before and after, bringing a virtual halt to population growth. This stability lasted from about 1590 to 1720 and beyond.[16] The Thirty Years' War (1618–48) emptied parts of the Germanies by either death or emigration. Spain and Italy suffered at least ten epidemics of plague and other diseases, and their populations fell. France was battered by periodic epidemics and famines. Plague swept London in 1665, killing perhaps a hundred thousand, according to Daniel Defoe's *Journal of the Plague Year*, which he wrote in 1721 when another epidemic crossed Europe (but spared England). Bad harvests deprived the poor and weakened their resistance to disease. Braudel called the period a "biological *ancien ré-gime*," whose marks were "balance between births and deaths, very high infant mortality, famine, chronic undernourishment and virulent epidemics. These oppressions hardly relaxed with the advances of the eighteenth century. . . ."[17]

England did not suffer all of the hardships that afflicted Europe, but the century still compared unfavorably to the eighteenth. Yet during the seventeenth century, Englishmen founded the colonies that in 1776 became the United States: the first in Virginia in 1607 and the last in Georgia in 1732, all in 125 years, the precise period when much of Europe and England were at their demographic worst since the disastrous, plague- and war-ridden fourteenth century. Population pressure by itself did not provoke colonization. The numbers of poor, and the expenditure needed to care for them, did rise in England in the late sixteenth and early seventeenth centuries, and in certain areas population was perceived by some to be overabundant.[18] But religion in New England and commerce in the Chesapeake were much more important motives for colonization. France, with 18 million people in 1600 to England's 4.5 million, sent her first colonists up the St. Lawrence about then, just a few years before Englishmen went to Virginia, Plymouth, and Boston. But the French colonists were even fewer than the English.

In the first years of most colonies, deaths outran births, and migration to them was a last resort of the destitute or spirit-struck. Population increased slowly if at all, especially in the southern colonies, for many reasons: Indian warfare, epidemics, malnutrition, a shortage of women, the cost of passage, rules against acquiring land and thus against forming a family, and a very sane fear of the howling wilderness.[19] The puzzling fecklessness of the first settlers at Jamestown, who according to reports preferred a short workday and playing games to raising the wheat essential for their survival, may have resulted from sheer malnutrition. In the first three years,

according to the newly-arrived Sir Thomas Gates, only sixty
men survived out of six hundred, and the sixty were almost
too weak to walk. The first years at Jamestown were truly
"starving times."[20] That was the worst case, but experiences of
other colonies in their earliest years suggest that desperation
had to be a motive for facing the ocean and the wilderness. In
the seventeenth century, England's North American colonies
were for the most part rude and fragile places, intrusions on
the edge of a vast empty land mass, put and kept there for
marginal economic advantage to their stockholders or propri-
etors or, in the case of the New England Puritans, because the
settlers were too quarrelsome to get along with the Crown, the
Church of England, or even with each other.[21] By 1700 the
total colonial population, from Maine to Georgia, was only
250,000.

Students of seventeenth-century America will doubtless
be outraged to be told that the century of Jamestown,
Plymouth, the Puritans, and so forth, is prehistory. But in a
demographic sense, it is. As Richard Hofstadter wrote, "So
many volumes have been written on the very earliest settlements that their bulk tends to conceal the important fact that
the population in these settlements was negligible in
number."[22] There were too few people, even at the close of the
seventeenth century, to interact in patterned ways, at least in
the frontier-rural pattern they would shortly exhibit and continue to exhibit for nearly two more centuries. New England's
early practice of settlement by town-congregation was weaken-
ing by the early eighteenth century, and did not survive long
beyond the Great Awakening and other events around 1740.
The plantations of the Chesapeake continued to exist, but
smallholdings far outnumbered them once native-born population began to increase by the end of the seventeenth century.
Demographically, the European-derived population of the
entire future United States was smaller than present-day
Winnipeg, Wyoming, or Wichita.[23] Granted, early New En-

gland had much more institutional impact than those places; demographic patterns are not the whole of history. But the evident facts that the early settlements grew very slowly, remained tiny, hugged the coastline, and depended for their social shape about as much on European ideas as on American realities and the possibilities which these settlements had yet to exploit,[24] separates them from the pervasive frontier-rural mode that was about to take shape, just as a prehistory is separate from a history.

Nevertheless it is worth a glance at New England and the Chesapeake in their seventeenth-century *Vorzeit* in order to see the differences they had with each other and with the frontier-rural mode to come, and in what ways they bore the seeds of that mode. From a demographic standpoint, early New England and the Chesapeake were very unlike eighteenth-century and later America. The first years at Jamestown were murderous: four out of five settlers in the first fifteen years died, and by 1624 the mortality rate was 252 per thousand (in the 1970s it was just under 9 per thousand in the United States). The crude death rate dropped to perhaps 35 to 55 per thousand in Maryland and Virginia in 1650–1700, and was somewhat lower (15 to 25) in Massachusetts by 1700. Life was short, especially in the Chesapeake.[25]

Vorzeit in the Chesapeake exhibited a very odd demographic regime by American standards. Such population increase as there was resulted from continued immigration, not from natural growth. It could hardly have been otherwise since the sex ratio was six males per female around 1650 and still about five to two in 1700. Indentured servitude, the condition of the majority of immigrants, delayed the age of marriage well into the twenties and thus reduced the number of children a couple would have, which was just as well since the average marriage lasted only seven years before one partner died. Infant and child mortality was high; almost half of those born would never see adulthood.[26] For the growing slave population the sex ratio was about 1.5 males per female, marriages were uncommon, and disease lowered the birth rate.[27]

The condition of women was unlike that in England or New England, or in the southern colonies later. If a woman survived her period of indenture, which was probably the condition under which she came to Maryland, she would almost certainly become the wife of a "planter," a male ex-indentured servant with a certain amount of land. The sex ratio almost guaranteed marriage for women. Premarital pregnancy was common (about one case in three, twice the incidence in England or New England), but the stigma was slight or absent if the couple married before the child was born. Women "were less protected but also more powerful than those who remained at home." On the other hand the death rate among women in the child-bearing years was higher than among men. High mortality afflicted slave women as well.[28]

For both men and women, life was shorter in the Chesapeake than in England at the same time, and if the localities so far researched represent the general pattern, "Most men who lived in Maryland in the early colonial period died well before they reached age fifty."[29] Only when a native-born generation came into being, which happened quite slowly, and when the native-born began to outnumber the English-born or African-born, which happened only after 1680 or 1700, did natural increase become rapid. Then the age of marriage fell, the sex ratio became less skewed, fertility rose, families formed, and the raising of children to adulthood became more normal. Native-born women did not arrive in Maryland under indenture and therefore could marry younger than their immigrant mothers. That brought more children, distributed normally as to sex. Marriage became more possible for the next generation of males. "By the mid-1680s, in all probability, the population thus began to grow through natural increase . . ." The same sort of thing happened to slaves, allowing for some degree of "stable family life" not present in the "isolating and dehumanizing experience" of slavery in the earliest decades.[30] In the Chesapeake, the turn of the seventeenth century into the eighteenth signaled the end of the *Vorzeit* as measured by demographic events.

New England also had its *Vorzeit* in the seventeenth century, but a different one. In fact, the outstanding differences between New England in the *Vorzeit* and the frontier-rural mode that became prevalent in the eighteenth and nineteenth century were less demographic, except for mobility, than social, specifically in social organization and settlement patterns. New England in the seventeenth century was a region of small, tightly knit communities, their civic form the town meeting and their religious form the congregation. The birth rate in Dedham, Massachusetts, for example, was about 40 per thousand, a little higher than in seventeenth-century French or English villages, and a little lower than in the United States at the end of the eighteenth century. The death rate, however, was considerably lower than in Europe: 27 per thousand compared to 30 or 40. People lived longer in New England than in the Chesapeake, often past fifty or even seventy. This, together with an average age of marriage of around twenty-two to twenty-four for women and twenty-five to twenty-seven for men, perhaps two years earlier than in Europe or the Chesapeake, and the high frequency of marriage, led to larger families, more rapid natural increase, and almost certainly more two-parent families during the childhood and adolescence of the offspring. In the early generations, when available property was still well beyond subsistence requirements, longer parental lives meant more parental control over children's marriages and inheritances.[31]

Mobility was very low in every sense except the method of establishing new towns, which was by clusters of families authorized to take up new land as a congregation. Immigration into New England in the seventeenth century (and much of the eighteenth) was meager after the first years. Emigration was also rare. In the case of Dedham, eight of ten people born there would live and die there, "still oblivious to the continent that waited to the westward."[32] Three features separating seventeenth- and early eighteenth-century New England from the Chesapeake and from the later frontier-rural mode appeared throughout Puritan New England from Maine to extreme southwestern Connecticut, where twenty-nine people founded Stamford in 1641:

> All were veterans of previous New England plantings, and all shared a commitment to the assumptions of non-separating Congregationalism, to the open field pattern of landholding, and to the system of autonomous community government that constituted the Puritan way of life in early Connecticut.[33]

The open-field economic system, with settlers living in a village community, encouraged them "to turn their backs on the wilderness," to stay put. Why not, as long as land was abundant? For most of the seventeenth century and beyond, towns usually had not fully cultivated their holdings.[34] The usual inheritance practice was to leave property equally to all children, with perhaps a double share to the oldest son.[35] This could not continue indefinitely, and in fact partible inheritance became rarer as land became scarcer and farms smaller by the third and fourth generations, that is, by the early eighteenth century. In eastern Massachusetts a man could acquire one or two hundred acres around 1650, but by the time of the American Revolution, the average farms in four towns near Boston were 56, 44, 38, and 17 acres. In Andover, the first generation bequeathed its property to all male heirs in 95 percent of the cases, but this was so of only 75 percent from second to third generation, 58 percent from third to fourth, and "less than half of the male members of the fourth Andover generation [maturing in the mid-eighteenth century] remained in the town for the rest of their lives." Some went into trades, some moved to other towns, some took up land elsewhere.[36]

Mobility out of the early towns thus increased in the eighteenth century as land became scarcer. The breakdown of the congregational communities had already begun, as farmers moved from the village to their increasingly distant farmlands. The original open-field, common land system was already breaking up by 1700 in some places.[37] Population rose rapidly in many towns. Women married later by a couple of years, a practice resulting in lower birth rates and declining family size (from 7.6 births per marriage in Andover in the 1690s to 5.7 in 1710–19 to 3.0 in 1785–94).[38] Mortality also rose and life expectancy decreased. The natural growth of New England's seventeenth-century population undermined its cherished congregational mode of settlement. Values, and the control of society by elites, were severely strained.[39] The Great Awakening, around 1740, further loosed the bonds of the congregation, as the population-conscious Ezra Stiles lamented:

> One source of different [anti-congregational] sentiment, were the unhappy excesses into which our churches have been transported in the late enthusiasm that prevailed since the year 1740. In the public mistaken zeal, religion was made to consist in extravigancies [sic] and indecencies, which were not according to the faith once delivered. Multitudes were seriously, soberly, and solemnly out of their wits.

That led to the forming of unauthorized assemblies, although a hundred and fifty authorized ones were also built, "not on the separations but natural increase."[40] Still, the *Vorzeit* was over in New England by the middle of the eighteenth century, often decades earlier. Massachusetts grew from 56,000 in 1700 to 91,000 in 1720, Connecticut from 26,000 in 1700 to 59,000 in 1720, straining the old ways past the breaking point. New Englanders either stayed in their sheltered towns, "old, stable, concentrated," and "clannish," or they looked at long last to frontier-rural opportunities.[41]

...aints among young New Englanders,[53] perhaps because re-
...urces permitted family formation more readily. For whatever
...of reasons, the American demographic regime was already
...ferent from Europe's. In James Cassedy's words,

...Operating with little restraint in an exceedingly favorable natural
...environment, human reproduction ultimately was sufficient to
...ensure a steady rise in population. By mid-18th century, with
...assistance from immigration, this growth had achieved what
...seemed to be an astonishing rate.[54]

The eighteenth-century sources on American population
...e scattered but consistent. Franklin wrote his *Observations*
...*cerning the Increase of Mankind* in 1751 and published it in
...55, to prove that Britain should allow colonial manufactur-
...g, since it was no threat to the mother country because co-
...nial consumers were getting so numerous. The tract is there-
...re tendentious, but some of its points are probably correct:

... Marriages in *America* are more general, and more generally
...early, than in *Europe*. And ... we may here reckon 8 [births per
...marriage compared to 4 in Europe], of which if one half grow
...up, and our Marriages are made, reckoning one with another at
...20 Years of Age, our People must at least be doubled every 20
...Years.[55]

...ra Stiles, writing in 1760, agreed. He estimated that New
...ngland's increase from a few thousand souls in 1643 to a half
...illion in 1760 was totally the result of natural increase, be-
...use "since that time more have gone from us to Europe, than
...ve arrived from thence hither." Stiles realized that net mi-
...ation, not gross, was the important number. Stiles also
...ticed that the interior grew faster than the coast: "The in-
...ease of the maritime towns is not equal to that of the inland
...es. ... While on the sea-coast it [the rate of doubling] is
...ove 25 years, yet within land it is 20 and 15."[56] Thus rural
...e and farming meant the fastest population growth. This
...rceptive observation was echoed in 1771 by Richard Price, a

The Emergence of the Frontier-Rural Mode

Between the 1720s and 1740s, the eighteenth century—in
demographic terms—started in Europe, and with it Europe's
great population explosion that was to last into the twentieth
century. Unlike the expansion of the sixteenth century, the
takeoff of the eighteenth century was not stopped by epidemic or
famine.[42] The reasons for the increase are not fully understood,
but falling death rates were a key element, because of the absence after 1720 of famines, epidemics, or wars like those of
the seventeenth century that ravaged civilian populations.[43]
Smallpox inoculation was widely practiced. Agriculture became more productive, at least in England, and the first signs
of industrialism appeared. With the development of markets,
towns and villages became more certain of sufficient food and
shelter to ensure survival and subsistence, which raised the
limits on reproduction. It was safer than before to have children. Birth rates rose while death rates kept dropping. England's population grew by about 300,000 in the first half of
the eighteenth century, by 3 million (from 6 to 9 million) in
the second. Much of this increase the industrializing English
economy could absorb, but some of it went to the colonies.
Their populations rose abruptly. The 250,000 of 1700 became
1,250,000 by 1750, or one colonist for every five people in
England. After 1750 the rate accelerated.

Who were these people, the American colonists? Immigration accounted for many, though it is impossible to say
how many. Benjamin Franklin, writing in 1751, estimated
"upwards of One million *English* souls in *North America* (tho'
'tis thought scarce 80,000 have been brought over Sea)."[44] This
estimate of immigrants seems low. A more likely figure is
200,000 English, and to that should be added an almost equal
number of Scotch-Irish, 100,000 Rhineland Germans, small
groups of French Huguenots, Swedes, Finns, and Sephardic

Jews, and at least 250,000 black Africans. By 1770, 21 percent of the whole population of the future United States were Africans or their descendants, virtually all slaves in the southern colonies: the highest proportion ever of black people. The total of immigrants (including Africans) between 1700 and 1775 was probably between 700,000 and 900,000, though the figures are obviously indefinite.

The scale of immigration may conjure up a mind's-eye view of eighteenth-century American population growth, a picture of ships disgorging boatload after boatload of Europeans on the docks of Boston or New York or Philadelphia, and Africans in Charleston and along the tidal rivers of Maryland, Virginia, and the Carolinas. We might picture, leaving out the Africans, the eastern seaboard filling up with an Anglo-Saxon, Protestant, freedom-loving, idealistic people fleeing European poverty and despotism. A handsome picture, but aside from the Anglo-Saxon Protestant part, a romantic one. The realities were that New England neither wanted nor got many immigrants. The only large non-British group other than the Africans were the Germans who settled in Pennsylvania between 1720 and 1750. Indisputably Protestant (Moravian, Reformed, or Lutheran), they nevertheless did not assimilate into the English majority. Franklin gave one reason in a comment he made in 1753. Though he favored intermarriage between English and German, or so he claimed, it was unlikely to happen.

> The German women are generally so disagreeable to an English eye, that it wou'd require great portions to induce Englishmen to marry them. Nor would the German Ideas of Beauty generally agree with our Women: *dick und starcke* . . . always enters into their Description of a pretty Girl.

Franklin was reputed to be an experienced judge.[45]

Our mind's-eye view errs also by not recognizing that most of the population increase in eighteenth-century America

was natural, the excess of births over death
fourth resulted from immigration,[46] and Fra
was less. For one thing, many who immigra
More important, natural increase was very rap
established by 1720. It was the most obvio
indicator of the frontier-rural mode of life.
from age twenty in New England was ab
years.[47] Smallpox inoculation among whites
cepted and practiced.[48] The death rate was mu
European cities such as Berlin, Paris, Breslau
the birth rate was surely much higher, and
death rates compared favorably to rural areas i
mortality was well below that of the cities. Po
survey of American population history befor
per-decade increases at 35 percent, with natu
counting for 26 to 30 percent.[50] Mortality wa
was short, but only by late twentieth-century
by the standards of eighteenth-century Eur
lived longer, married younger, had more chil
of them live to maturity, than Europeans did.

As a result of this natural increase, the
onists passed 1 million sometime in the 1740
was a relatively slow decade. By the time the
independence from England in 1776, they nun
million, one for every three English men an
slow or negative growth of the *Vorzeit* had bee
new demographic regime marked by very ra
crease. Once the American population approa
size, say the 250,000 of 1700, it looked nothin
tional regime of Europe before the "demograph
It already enjoyed lower mortality and higher
between rates of births and deaths which wou
population to grow even without any immigrati
instances of premarital conception of the first c
eighteenth century, perhaps because of crum

The Emergence of the Frontier-Rural Mode

Between the 1720s and 1740s, the eighteenth century—in demographic terms—started in Europe, and with it Europe's great population explosion that was to last into the twentieth century. Unlike the expansion of the sixteenth century, the takeoff of the eighteenth century was not stopped by epidemic or famine.[42] The reasons for the increase are not fully understood, but falling death rates were a key element, because of the absence after 1720 of famines, epidemics, or wars like those of the seventeenth century that ravaged civilian populations.[43] Smallpox inoculation was widely practiced. Agriculture became more productive, at least in England, and the first signs of industrialism appeared. With the development of markets, towns and villages became more certain of sufficient food and shelter to ensure survival and subsistence, which raised the limits on reproduction. It was safer than before to have children. Birth rates rose while death rates kept dropping. England's population grew by about 300,000 in the first half of the eighteenth century, by 3 million (from 6 to 9 million) in the second. Much of this increase the industrializing English economy could absorb, but some of it went to the colonies. Their populations rose abruptly. The 250,000 of 1700 became 1,250,000 by 1750, or one colonist for every five people in England. After 1750 the rate accelerated.

Who were these people, the American colonists? Immigration accounted for many, though it is impossible to say how many. Benjamin Franklin, writing in 1751, estimated "upwards of One million *English* souls in *North America* (tho' 'tis thought scarce 80,000 have been brought over Sea)."[44] This estimate of immigrants seems low. A more likely figure is 200,000 English, and to that should be added an almost equal number of Scotch-Irish, 100,000 Rhineland Germans, small groups of French Huguenots, Swedes, Finns, and Sephardic

Jews, and at least 250,000 black Africans. By 1770, 21 percent of the whole population of the future United States were Africans or their descendants, virtually all slaves in the southern colonies: the highest proportion ever of black people. The total of immigrants (including Africans) between 1700 and 1775 was probably between 700,000 and 900,000, though the figures are obviously indefinite.

The scale of immigration may conjure up a mind's-eye view of eighteenth-century American population growth, a picture of ships disgorging boatload after boatload of Europeans on the docks of Boston or New York or Philadelphia, and Africans in Charleston and along the tidal rivers of Maryland, Virginia, and the Carolinas. We might picture, leaving out the Africans, the eastern seaboard filling up with an Anglo-Saxon, Protestant, freedom-loving, idealistic people fleeing European poverty and despotism. A handsome picture, but aside from the Anglo-Saxon Protestant part, a romantic one. The realities were that New England neither wanted nor got many immigrants. The only large non-British group other than the Africans were the Germans who settled in Pennsylvania between 1720 and 1750. Indisputably Protestant (Moravian, Reformed, or Lutheran), they nevertheless did not assimilate into the English majority. Franklin gave one reason in a comment he made in 1753. Though he favored intermarriage between English and German, or so he claimed, it was unlikely to happen.

> The German women are generally so disagreeable to an English eye, that it wou'd require great portions to induce Englishmen to marry them. Nor would the German Ideas of Beauty generally agree with our Women: *dick und starcke* . . . always enters into their Description of a pretty Girl.

Franklin was reputed to be an experienced judge.[45]

Our mind's-eye view errs also by not recognizing that most of the population increase in eighteenth-century America was natural, the excess of births over deaths. Perhaps one-fourth resulted from immigration,[46] and Franklin thought it was less. For one thing, many who immigrated did not stay. More important, natural increase was very rapid and was well established by 1720. It was the most obvious demographic indicator of the frontier-rural mode of life. Life expectancy from age twenty in New England was about forty more years.[47] Smallpox inoculation among whites was widely accepted and practiced.[48] The death rate was much lower than in European cities such as Berlin, Paris, Breslau, and Vienna,[49] the birth rate was surely much higher, and both birth and death rates compared favorably to rural areas in Europe, where mortality was well below that of the cities. Potter's pioneering survey of American population history before 1860 set total per-decade increases at 35 percent, with natural increase accounting for 26 to 30 percent.[50] Mortality was high and life was short, but only by late twentieth-century standards, not by the standards of eighteenth-century Europe. Americans lived longer, married younger, had more children, saw more of them live to maturity, than Europeans did.

As a result of this natural increase, the number of colonists passed 1 million sometime in the 1740s, although that was a relatively slow decade. By the time they declared their independence from England in 1776, they numbered over 2.5 million, one for every three English men and women. The slow or negative growth of the *Vorzeit* had been replaced by a new demographic regime marked by very rapid natural increase. Once the American population approached significant size, say the 250,000 of 1700, it looked nothing like the traditional regime of Europe before the "demographic transition."[51] It already enjoyed lower mortality and higher fertility, a gap between rates of births and deaths which would have caused population to grow even without any immigration.[52] Recorded instances of premarital conception of the first child rose in the eighteenth century, perhaps because of crumbling social re-

straints among young New Englanders,[53] perhaps because resources permitted family formation more readily. For whatever
set of reasons, the American demographic regime was already
different from Europe's. In James Cassedy's words,

> Operating with little restraint in an exceedingly favorable natural
> environment, human reproduction ultimately was sufficient to
> ensure a steady rise in population. By mid-18th century, with
> assistance from immigration, this growth had achieved what
> seemed to be an astonishing rate.[54]

The eighteenth-century sources on American population
are scattered but consistent. Franklin wrote his *Observations
concerning the Increase of Mankind* in 1751 and published it in
1755, to prove that Britain should allow colonial manufactur-
ing, since it was no threat to the mother country because colonial consumers were getting so numerous. The tract is therefore tendentious, but some of its points are probably correct:

> . . . Marriages in *America* are more general, and more generally
> early, than in *Europe*. And . . . we may here reckon 8 [births per
> marriage compared to 4 in Europe], of which if one half grow
> up, and our Marriages are made, reckoning one with another at
> 20 Years of Age, our People must at least be doubled every 20
> Years.[55]

Ezra Stiles, writing in 1760, agreed. He estimated that New
England's increase from a few thousand souls in 1643 to a half
million in 1760 was totally the result of natural increase, because "since that time more have gone from us to Europe, than
have arrived from thence hither." Stiles realized that net migration, not gross, was the important number. Stiles also
noticed that the interior grew faster than the coast: "The increase of the maritime towns is not equal to that of the inland
ones. . . . While on the sea-coast it [the rate of doubling] is
above 25 years, yet within land it is 20 and 15."[56] Thus rural
life and farming meant the fastest population growth. This
perceptive observation was echoed in 1771 by Richard Price, a